THE HUM HEARERS

Shey Marque

Shey Marque is an award-winning writer and former medical scientist from Western Australia. She holds a BAppSc(Hons), PhD Molecular Pathology, and MA Writing. Shey developed a special interest in epigenetics and inheritance of cellular memory while researching molecular genetics during her PhD at the University of Western Australia. This collection examines those concepts in the context of family history. Shey's work has been published nationally and internationally in journals, choreographed for contemporary dance, and made into short poetry film. Her poetry has won awards including the Blue Nib Chapbook Award, a QLD Poetry Festival Emerging Poet Award, Poetry d'Amour Prize, KSP Poetry Prize, runner-up for the Gwen Harwood Poetry Prize, Bruce Dawe Poetry Prize, and shortlisted for others including the Tom Collins Prize, Ros Spencer Prize, MPU Poetry Prize, ACU Literature Prize, the Noel Rowe Award, and the Dorothy Hewett Award. Her previous books are *Aporiac* (Finishing Line Press, USA, 2016), and *Keeper of the Ritual* (UWAP 2019). *The Hum Hearers* is her third collection.

THE HUM HEARERS

Shey Marque

U W
A P
UWA PUBLISHING

First published in 2025 by
UWA Publishing
Crawley, Western Australia 6009
www.uwap.uwa.edu.au

UWAP is an imprint of UWA Publishing
a division of The University of Western Australia

THE UNIVERSITY OF
WESTERN
AUSTRALIA

ISBN: 978-1-76080-300-1

NATIONAL
LIBRARY
OF AUSTRALIA
A catalogue record for this
book is available from the
National Library of Australia

Cover design by Hazel Lam
Typeset in Joanna Nova by Lasertype
Printed by Lightning Source

uwapublishing

CELEBRATING
UWAP 90 YEARS

CONTENTS

INTRODUCTION

The Hum Hearers explores the post-genomic entanglement between the body and environment through epigenetic inheritance, or cellular memory. What is epigenetics? Instead of thinking about the genome as a fixed blueprint to construct a body, we can think of it as a piece of literature. Like a book, it can be read and interpreted in different ways. There is growing scientific evidence that environment and the memory of experience, seen most readily with traumatic events such as war and genocide (Perroud et al. 334), impacts our DNA with the effects transferred to future generations.

One of my favourite studies has shown that 'memory' of trauma and fear can be inherited. In a classic experiment (Dias and Ressler 89), mice conditioned to fear the scent of cherry blossom gave rise to descendants which exhibited the same fear without being conditioned. Similarly, humans who are descendants of holocaust survivors exhibit elevated stress responses compared to control populations. This carryover to future generations could explain the increasing incidence of mental illness and stress disorder among us, as well as the increasing volatility of the world. Interestingly, research also suggests that inheritance of genetic 'tags' is not necessarily permanent and can be reversed (Phelps and Hofmann 43). I hope we can learn how to do this.

We are essentially a symphony of particles and light, an energy that's never destroyed, only transformed, and can transcend space and time (Einstein's 'spooky action at a distance'). Our DNA carries a vibrational energy (I'm calling it the hum), measurable by experiment, which may be influenced by distant triggers (Backster and White 132). These observations fit into current theories of quantum physics and the fourth dimension (quantum entanglement). These beliefs are not altogether new, though. For example, American Indians believe that everything we do will not only affect the seven generations to come, but also the preceding seven generations, which implies that the generations past, present and future could co-exist on an energetic level in a space-time continuum (Rich np).

With all this in mind, I set about to trace family memory by following the women in my mother's line back to Victorian London. My research uncovered a history that begins in a music hall in Covent Garden, *Evans Music and Supper Rooms* at 43 King St, owned by my maternal forefather John (Paddy) Green from 1842. His wife Sarah, daughter Jessie Green (Bebb) and the lives of all the women descended from her, inspired the poems in this collection. Illness like cholera and tuberculosis, bankruptcy, abandonment, migration, war and domestic violence were some of the traumatic events identified through the generations.

In the midst of writing, a sad trajectory emerged. My mother was diagnosed unexpectedly with the aggressive and incurable brain tumour, glioblastoma, passing away in 2022 and bringing an end to her own memories. The ones not yet recovered are perhaps residing somewhere within me. I dedicate this collection to her.

SM

'...the thing I run from rides on my back and in my blood and will not be shaken'— Intisar Khanani

Unberthed

Look up. Consider the word *incubus*. Freeze while it manifests internal textures. The movie scene dangles on its exploratory thread from the ceiling. Close your mouth. Stick out your hand. Touch the other side of the bed just to check it's empty. Listen to the scrape of stainless steel on granite, a dog whimper. Fill the stove-top espresso maker with caramel arabica. Swat a fly with the tea towel. Watch those nuts, seeds & psyllium husks turn into neat buns. Instant message a friend who doesn't waste time on punctuality. She knows tomorrow is Wednesday. Put the bins out. Become absorbed in *Belief*[1]. Find *Perspective* on page twenty one. Play back a message from your mother. When you ask, she says she remembers a fine web beyond the theatre light in the birthing room, & the hope that the little spider doesn't fall as she delivers you face upwards. Breathe.

---

1 *Belief* (Flying Islands 2018), Les Wicks

Instinction

I was two days old when my mother left me in a pram outside Stammers & went home. She said she felt oddly lighter though it took a while to realise what was missing. Nobody noticed me. I might have been a window. For those twenty minutes the separation slipped by me. Mum was on her knees scrubbing floors in a convent by age seven. Her mother had been left in an orphanage & so it goes. Back to coda. You left a daughter with nuns & sailed away on your violin. So many women with habits that would never be broken. Minnie was the one who put my grandmother in an orphanage, ran around town with a gangster. He caught her fear by the hair, shot it through the temple. How carelessly/joyously she was shedding her religion. I grew up with an irrational fear of nuns the way my dog always ran when I so much as reached for a violin. He saw right through me that morning as he watched me pack & leave my first husband. I know how I'm marked, how I can vanish.

Lost Wax

for Jessie Green (Bebb)

I'm gluing together a tiny violin, its edges melting with the touch of a lit match. I've traced and excised all the parts with painstaking precision. Each panel aligns and the join sets quickly as the wax cools. The liquid spreads, grows over the cuts like new skin. A thin stream of vapour rises as if a candle snuffed only a moment ago, and the scent of hot throw makes me sleepy. I want to climb the staircase at West Hall, with this replica instrument on my outstretched palm, my other hand feeling for the banister to keep upright in the dark. At the top of the stairs your door might be open and I could walk right in, leave this model on your pillowcase for casting in the way of Theophilus and his bells. If by chance the lost wax should infiltrate your skin, I could section you on my microtome with its tempered blade, fix you to a glass slide (lace- thin so as to let the light in), maybe see a reflection of myself through the little window.

Untimely Fruit

A seer once said to me *there is a child here asking to come, but he'll go away if you tell him*. It was a spirit baby, unossified, breathing through a hollow of skin. I mouthed the word *fontanelle*, felt its soft give. He was never more than that pulsating space. At seventeen I got a part-time job in a bookshop, saved two hundred dollars, kept the cash in a secret place should I cease to become unwell. A friend of a friend said that was the cost—a safety net, if hours of dancing in clubs, riding horses, carrying typewriters couldn't dislodge the pretzel. Nights of pubs, parties, concerts, coming home in the small hours through fog & rain, fevered, overexcited, too tired to wake in the morning was the fashion. Chevasse, in his *advice to a wife*, called fashion just another name for suicide, baby slaughter, a massacre of the innocents. Such women could never keep a bird in the cage. I wanted to be a bird without a cage. You wanted to be a cage without a bird. Laced in your waist to twenty-two inches, practised controlled falls down a flight of stairs, sat in hot baths, swallowed pills of aloe, ginger & soap, from a bottle that carried the warning *must not be used while pregnant*.

Let me run a salt bath for her, burn some sage, chant

(im) Jane Cooling Munday, Oxfordshire 1851, and her sons who all died from
Friedreich's Ataxia

I am descended from song, song-givers, horsehair perukes, square & compass, ichthys. I am the thrower of hooks into a timeless air. Today we pause, my cousin & I, to cast voice from the riverbank. A right-eyed sole flops out of the water, attaches itself to his foot—one without sensation. We are falling back to where someone else is falling forward. It's a woman getting baptised in the Thames, born in the wrong, waiting to be put right. She takes on a new name, a foreign accent, eats cucumber ice cream on the way home. The icecream drops on the road. Rain washes it into a pothole. Left eye clouded over, she's at Jane's wedding where the bride's derogatory remarks land on her like a slap. She points a finger, *may the limbs of all male offspring in your lineage wither and die.* The woman opens her kiln, fires curse into art. At home she drops a ceramic urn on slate tiles. The urn collapses into a hundred intersecting arcs.

Taking photos of strangers after breakfast in the crypt

Number 6, rue de Fourcy

History doesn't always stay where you think you left it. On occasion it follows you up the stairs to your rented room, smells of frankincense, drops candle wax or a prayer book. A homeless woman fetches the price of a good meal, doors open and close all night. Convent, house of tolerance, hostel; the place is all these things at once. Every room the same; single beds wrapped in white cotton sheets, a shower & wash basin, but you have to wander the corridor to find a place to pee. Maybe this was her room. Outside in the cloister, underneath the covered walkway, is a geranium hanging over an old stone fountain. I sit there, touch walls she might have touched. *Au petit feu a cheval* presses coffee, makes the best hot chocolate in the Marais, so thick you don't need cake. I was never sure whether it was they learning my language or me learning theirs. Child on a bicycle looks into backscatter of particles and light with me as artefact, features superimposed. I force my face into a new expression & it stays for now. Tomorrow she'll climb out of me again.

Autumn at West Hall

A horse-drawn bus carries you through London. You can't stop thinking of the many flowers that refuse to grow, or those men who wander blind through pea soup, fall into the Thames. Your mother won't leave the house anymore. She's inhaled a song, a tiny germ of which has rendered her breathless. Still you sing, tread sodden leaf to the door of the house, its walls layered with soot & virgin ivy. Wonder at the Plane tree cleaning itself in the courtyard. How both of you shed your blackened coats. You squint so as to keep out the fog, keep the path in focus. If I be skelly like that I can almost unblur you.

Bathing in vinegar & leftover wine

Downstairs, men and children are sharing water in the tin bath tub beside the fire, eldest to youngest. Water becomes so dirty you could lose small children, so alive you could fish in it. Women are not willing to be naked in the kitchen. She is upstairs in the bedroom having a stand-up wash from the jug, a cloth wet with water warmed in the kettle, a splash of vinegar. On a mat woven from worn-out clothes, she pours water from the pitcher into a porcelain bowl. Lilies & leaves hand painted in flow blue, tiny hairline in the glaze. Nightdress lifted waist high, her hand runs a wet flannel under arms, in creases between belly & thigh. A woman's groin is a shelter for fish, a funnel to net them, a wharf, a landing place. While she bathes, she sings to herself *au clair de la lune*, splits a photon.

six of us wash in the same bathwater
laced with blue nun
a brother makes armpit jazz

Liaison at Evans' Music Hall

Celebrity portraits line walls of the conversation cafe. They wink, quip behind cupped hands. Dim light keeps you looking over your shoulder. From the upstairs gallery you throw flowers over the edge onto the stage. On occasion you sit head-to-head with a lover—for the sake of handed-down gossip, call him Bertie. He takes off his top hat, leans on an elbow, rests a polished shoe casually behind the other, candid for the camera. But he's budgie-eyed like his mother. You risk a bite.

Sunset Salad

At a faraway café, he leans over the balcony to pick an angel's trumpet and says, for you. He orders herring bones, I want edible flowers. There's nothing dangerous about the calendula or nasturtium. We nibble on some, press a few into my diary, take a selfie. Once our champagne glasses are empty, we cradle strawberries, cleaving little hearts in two, check for sharpness.

Clannad

Your hair is a three-ply flower braid, twisted, unravelled. His is a russet pelt of foxglove laid on white sheet. He's an overdose of Digitalis. Each poisoning makes your weakened heart work harder. Leather, ambergris & perianth press against skin, become interstitial. The rose's thorns are shaved, but what consequences of a stem broken by excess? He abandons Friday in its frenetic final minutes, rises to leave. The air around him speeds up, petals lift for a second. You roll back onto them, fall asleep. By morning they will flatten into wounds.

Shooting Cloud at a Sky

for *Charles Herbert Bebb*

i

In a political economy of love, the arrival of children was often associated with the loss of a flatterer's affection and eventual disappearance of happiness. Of course, there came mistresses – there was always some actress, Danish princess or the errant wife of a Lord. After the quickening, you were left with a scrap and the makings of a boy out of opera, smog and tonic wine. Who knew he'd weave those into hotels, opera houses and love for large cities? I have a picture of him that you would never have seen, face like his father's, sac of architecture slung low over his right hip, rifle in his hands, shooting cloud at a sky teeming with birdly houses. (I suppose it's a play on the clay pigeon, a reference to the ceasing of his passion for terra cotta ornament.) Those miniature brick buildings on wing, the only little angels he'd ever have. That germ of you residing in him was also remaindered in me.

ii

Well yes I loved, and from those I loved I ran, I ran first, I ran early. I thought I could outwit rejection as if it might pass by me like a sniper while I hid under the desk in a schoolroom. To all of the physical walls that contained me, all the windows I had modified into doors so that I could line up a sudden escape from wherever I stood. To all the empty sacs, the reversible cartilage, the resorption of three hundred soft bones, and the shrinking tails of incipients that never were. Forgive me.

The Art of Savouring Her Imperfections

'Suddenly she stopped, clutched her throat and a wave of crimson blood ran down her breast…It rendered her even more ethereal', Poe, 1842

He was splitting a pigeon with his wife. She stifled a cough but none of that mattered. That way he looked upon the rise and fall of her cage, those bird shoulders a perfect symmetry of acromion & coracoids from which a sprouting of wings might be hinged. She hovered over her plate, twitching, nibbling at a tiny version of herself. A fine spidering of blue just below the surface of her skin, a net of vessels keeping her stitched together. Behind them on the dresser, a blue ceramic bowl once smashed into a thousand pieces, glued back together with a lacework of resin & powdered gold. For a long moment she was still, fork poised in the air as though thinking to say something important.

If a Flower Could be Called a Waif

for Sarah Green

Sarah was in the flowering of her age, rose for a mouth, belladonna eyes. Fashion watered her. You can grow an icon just like her. Take a ribbon of white silk, fray the top, bone the whole thing with a network of fine sugar-wire. Watch her dissolve slowly in bad air. Hippocrates would have fed her on asses' milk while she wasted away in a temple. Galen would give her a meal of wolf liver, elephant urine, & a sea voyage in favourable winds. She was tubercular chic with her wasp waist & voluminous skirt. How all their friends envied her pale skin, limpid eyes, stung lips. I bleach my hair, waxen my face. Something in my code wants to paint over my veins in vivid blue so as to frail my skin to porcelain. My body no longer wants me to eat. Therapeutic attempts at reversal can't yet shake this tag from my cells. In all my favourite photos I'm overexposed.

How to Forget Everything

after *The Ratcatcher's Daughter*, Samuel Cowell, 1844

On stage he moved bohemian style in half steps, half tempo, and for a pound a week plus whisky he sang of a Westminster girl, a ratcatcher's daughter. How her red hair dangled as if a bunch of carrots and she carried on her head a pile of small herring. The one time I ended up with carrot hair was after singing in the bathroom of an Invercargill nightclub that smelled of old fish. Shots were free, the DJ was hot and we danced like Shakira. At lesser ale houses rowdy men from the floor shouted to the performers, threw bottles and old boots on stage, and once a dead cat, at the point where the girl falls into the river, her mind apparently filled with lily-white sand. Despite the noise he continued telling of the rat-catcher's daughter because her drowning was not the end of the song and the audience would cheer at the point where her lover opened his throat with an edge of glass in that way heroes do, and the broken-hearted. He would have bled out through that casual tracheotomy, his useless fish mouth opening anyway. The crowd had understood him to be ruined when all he could have wanted was diversion, a temporary means to escape pain—like I might dig fingernails into flesh around a raw wound. After the stricken couple were stilled and there was no-one left to sing about, suddenly every man looked better to himself. When my singing was done I taxied home in the snow and brushed my teeth in freezing water. It made me forget my head.

To the Bone

Phossies never need worry about the sun. Light is coloured dust hanging in the air, settling on walls and factory floors, and where light falls upon a wall becomes transparent like a veil[1]. White phosphorus gets caught up in your hair, on your clothes, and your mouth goes green in the dark just from breathing. All you ever wanted was to feel a warm hand on your back, some safe place to sleep away from the damp, a hot potato. After a while it's the only thing soft enough to eat, what with the toothache and swelling of gums. Of course, it's the children who get picked because they're cheap to feed and fold up easily in a tight space. About that they'd say nothing if only they could grow some teeth, or an entire jaw, be able to eat again for just one more day.

Note: 'Phossies' refers to match factory workers in the nineteenth century who developed phossy jaw, a necrosis of the jaw, as a result of white phosphorus poisoning.

1 'The Little Match Girl', Hans Christian Andersen, 1845

Arguments Yard

This dry afternoon of April, this harbour grey light, sees her hang laundry on the wooden railing of the laneway stairs. She does it one-handed, the other resting on a hip, her yawn wide like a scream as children simulate a quarrel in the foreground. I notice there isn't any sound. Neighbours pause a while under the Spring sun—nobody knows I'm here, except for a man leaning on a windowsill, watching me watching her work. She, white- aproned, beats skin cells out of bedding, and a floor rug, balancing on the stairs, one foot on the lower step, the other one on the landing, short-sleeved long dress hiding her shoes, hair pinned back but shedding. Sandstone-walled houses surround the courtyard, each window a composite of tiny glass panes hard to clean in the corners. Our feet have been walking away with the top surface of the walkway for centuries. At street level the wooden outhouse in the corner by the stairs takes centre focus, it's a gateway for the passing of existences.

Out of Failing Bodies

Years from now there will be someone trying to reassemble my life from old photographs. They'll get the order of things wrong. I'm a muddled text. Hewoevr the mldide of my lfie is not irnomtapt so lnog as the bininnegg and einndg is crcreot. I played around with time a lot, played for time, rarely played in the pocket. A friend is close to the end of his life so I put him on the moon, had him dance at the Moulin Rouge. He became Pope, flew like a birdman. Right now, if I had her photo, I'd cut and paste her next to me in a digital re-creation. Maybe a relative not yet born will Photoshop me so that I fit right into some family portrait of the future. I'm looking back six generations at an image so unclear she continues to morph before my mind's eye. Three percent of my code once belonged to her. Soon she'll disappear forever. My DNA could hang around for six more generations. Or maybe I will leave a complete map of me frozen in a test tube, reappear, start over. I'll no longer know my limit, or what dying means.

Inhabiting the tesseract

Between our adjacent rooms the voile twitches liminal, exposes the perpendicular. We are entangled, she & I, the way in which nothing really dies, woven into the same fabric of the next dimension. Living side by side in *the crooked house*, beans are still sliced on the diagonal, spilt salt flung over the left shoulder. As for that singing, stringing in my ear at night—is it really just tinnitus? I want to go where the sun circles continuous in the same summer sky & time is whatever you want it to be, nothing   but our photons splitting. On those days I see my skin is not an impenetrable barrier, but a net with tiny holes through which even that stranger on the street gets in. I've started holding in my breath around anybody I don't want to inhale. The air in here is so thick with voice now, the walls cannot contain us, & as the house folds in on itself I can catch the wail of all her quantum daughters leaping out of windows.

Tracings

What if you could reach into your chromosomes and touch them in that intrinsic place where they rattle off a list of instructions left behind by generations long gone? Say you try to join them, end to end, to reconstruct the messenger, find some instructions too difficult to make out, misreckoned like an errant translation into English. Instead of finding the blueprint to an insight, you might find half each of two blueprints, like cutting a flatworm in half after which the tail end grows another tail and the head grows another head. You discover other reconstructed boo-boos, ex-genes, parasitic sequences, viral bones and belly-button lint. What if nucleic squatters signal old impulses, those contradictory ones that nobody knew how to stop, persisting as a carry-over? Like the viral parasite that wakes unbidden in your genetic bed, making copies of itself just for its own sake, you find an ancestor often wants nothing other than to say *don't forget me, don't forget me.*

Kandinskyesque

Looking into the operating microscope, I hold the tiniest pair of stainless-steel forceps, and within them sits a mouse calf *anterior tibialis*. I just move my hands. *The artist is the hand that plays.* I squeeze once then let him go. In twenty minutes he'd be awake and I wonder whether he'd dreamed he was dying, if he could see himself in all my dangerous paintings; a string of anxious forms, co-dependent, no life of their own once separated from each other. My electron micrographs show synaptic clefts as the curving lines of a foaming shoreline, tailing waves; an axon terminus as smooth pebbles and rocky outcrops at the foot of the dunes; and a sarcomere recognisable vaguely and fleetingly as an offshore coral reef, a scattering of fishing vessels. I'm down on the monochrome beach, teeming with endless seashells, water-eroded stones, and floating weed. There are oddly-shaped eyes everywhere. Surrealists could liken a nucleus to a beach ball or the sun, add a rush of childhood memories. Yes I can hear the tide, smell the salt, this little world inside a world inside a world.

Any Skin but Our Own

I lean into her winged mirror. On the dresser, the girl in a box still dances to Für Elise. Inside, a tangle of sticky pearls. Spit will tackle the grime from someone's little fingers & if I glance them off the tip of my nose, the oil will add sheen. On some other day we could be shelling peas together in the kitchen, careful to avoid the sort of mess we never talk about. An urge to roll those perfect spheres over tongue, across teeth, bite down until the strand breaks & fifty flawed pearls spill to the boards. Paring back to the intimacy of shedding, I cut into one, peel off the outer layer, rub over scratches with a fine powder of shell. The naked eye would barely see the blemish, its cover-girl skin glowing as I hold it up against a deepening sky. *Come away from the window. Tonight's moon could drown this pearl in its own light,* her voice closing like a hug, or a kind of squeezing.

Old Man Who Spits Pearls

case study in The Journal of Geriatric Mental Health, *Agarwal et al, 2018*

Coming from a family of oyster farmers, there's pearl in his blood, tumbling arterial. Even the sound of the word is organic, the shape of it in your mouth, fleshly. One day he begins spitting pearls, rolling them across tongue, body, bed sheet & blanket, tracking them as they travel under the skin. He rubs over & over with thumbs, clearing the budding from every pore. Day by day he changes the bed, washes his clothes, to rid them of the beaded infestation. Doctors gather head-to-head to watch the undulations in his throat, the incessant swallowing & coughing to work loose the pearls from his lungs. All this makes you question whether you'd come down with something if you were to walk into a sneezing of bead. You imagine catching pearls. Imagine pearl as parasite.

Triptych with Oranges

i

The valley cambered as much as hollowed between hills that let us come here as strangers dropping flesh around planted fields, a containment where the orchard coughed up oranges, forsaken fruit that nobody picked. One by one they fell, each swollen ovary from a single blossom, rolling downhill until stopped & co-located at the lowest corner of the rusted steel- wire fence, like a massive fermenting neon arrowhead pointing to the river where it hugged the coat a leafless tree was trying to pull under.

ii

You always said neon when you meant luminescent, started painting watercolour trees on cardboard back when you were single and deep, working away in the East. You came home stung by the colour orange & exhausted ironwood jungles. Woods separated you from the street – its names, eyes, spit & fur, the cluster of man passing, playing. I remember you sitting at the Blackbutt table, dining on glow, blooded moon crashing into the house, you licking it from the polished blade of a knife.

iii

We crossed the main road in the suburb's south, passing its pile of broken tables on the verge, its row of never-opened windows. The smoke-wracked air stung even our spit as it left our mouths. You obsessed over there not being enough names for orange, how each related back to edible things – apricot, tangerine, salmon. *Hear how the rainwater sounds just like the sea in the gully where the street meets the sidewalk.* I said it only to distract. You coughed, lifted a traffic cone, and held it to your ear, nodding.

Under the weight of an anencephalic moon

after Charles Joseph Martin

every reckoning finds its nesting place in some dark corner. if he keeps very still, he can feel it crossing perpendiculars. there is always that old wound to bring a person undone. interstitial like vernacular, it enters, rearranges him, spreads the particulate scar & he ends up a less coherent version of what he could have been. he'll come home drunk then wake the girls at two am to make him a cup of tea. they listen while he picks a fight over the way she makes the bed, how dinner is too much of one thing & not enough of another, & his pajamas aren't comfortable. she locks herself in the bedroom while his argument loses itself inside his toothless mouth & Glaswegian accent. he pauses to throw china at the walls. teenage daughters look at each other, wink, ask him endless questions to which the answer can only be *orrrranges*.

A cow and the chickens are out back

The goat's in the kitchen again, hind legs on a stool, forelegs on the table. It's eating the plastic curtains. Charlie is head-down beside the goat, sleeping off the whisky. There are forty-four scars to be counted, stitched from belly to chest, through a hole in his freshly-chewed shirt. A pouch of rough-cut Log Cabin tobacco, about to fall from his trouser pocket, is pinched by two young boys. Crouched behind the outhouse, hatbands bulging with the shredded, cured leaves which they'd seen him suck on or smoke wrapped in strips of old newspaper, a smoldering match sets the dead grass alight.

Doing bird in their bedroom, the best view for hours is a brick herringbone wall of the cottage adjacent. Through the boys' keyhole, the russet iron door key rests on a table. Let out for dinner, they complain about the stringy meat being too tough to chew. You're kidding, he says, still sucking.

A Sum of Spectacles[1]

'The grandiloquent truth of gestures...' – Baudelaire

It was the one thing they had in common, the one night she got to stay up late. At nine o'clock father & daughter were listening to a wrestling broadcast on the valve radio in its large wooden cabinet, with an old car battery for a power source. Her goldfish swam upside down, played dead, as the commentator's word theatre filled the living room with comedy & tragi-drama. Big Chief Little Wolf was busy throwing some fine upstanding fellow about the ropes, held him in that Indian Deadlock, performing warrior torture. *'Cept in a pretzel-bending factory you can't get more tangled up than this!* Sounds of grunting & straining made her father shout & cheer. Because her goldfish hadn't pooped in days, she poached tiny peas while she listened, squeezed them from their shells. *He can't get out of it. He can't get out of it. He's out of it!* Father leapt to his feet, kicked himself free & when he punched the air with his fist she ducked. *Big Chief patrolling the ring, long feathered headdress flowing.* Fish chased its pea to the bottom of the tank, tailfins fanning.

1 Barthes, Roland. 'The World of Wrestling.' *Mythologies*. New York: Hill and Wang, 1972.

Sequelae to misplaced elbows and other violations

i
The man who takes *tea* in a laddie dram glass,
despite his take-no-shit nose, does
seem less at ease in this country, or not even,
has closed down the dogs, getting drunk
      on needing to hurt the flesh
how it wipes him of ducking in the Clyde,
days in the hull, but it's done already, and he lives
              only on retribution and a rear view
confused over time, trying
to pin down something beyond recall

ii
The nightly crusade for unwronging
two small boys – the not quite angels –
knees to boards, a scant definition of bodies
      hovering beside him, prayer hands
angled bones, their hinges canting
      toward what could be the absence of a table
until finally he sleeps, shoulder to shoulder
with their mother who doesn't and there's no telling
how repletely a two-o'clock city spreads
its dark across the room

iii
Twin shapes of shame just hanging there
suddenly too much to bear, she'll unbend them
from the floor ridden cold and blind-
    walk them back to bed
catching little toes on the corner of the stairs
but at this hour all screaming is done
on the inside, exiting
through waggling hands, nothing is spoken
at the breakfast table – it's difficult to eat
    arms rope-tied to a chair

iv
A swig of tea, the swallowing, the swallow's wing
in her throat, like a loose stitch
undoes the gravity, the imperative, the eye –
    all those unfunny things
are pulling silly faces in the wrong moment. Caught
in quick dissolve to domestic actuality
the morning tastes not of charred bread and dripping
    but nicotined fingers and metal
her hands closing over her face, while he reads
the light as it curls like butter in the diaphanous air

F(l)ight
for Philip and Charles

Brothers had wounds like centipedes, filleting blade passing through the lamp-lit evening from which they fell, clattering over the ground like two dinner plates, a door banging, a broom wandering the porches, puncturing heaven.

On the bus, a beating, wheezing anatomy, and scent of bubble-gum rising from the bench seat. Reflections in the window were deaf. What was said was never said. It remained inside everything they heard – the blade, the broom, the banging.

Always Running

I am the bearer of your unuttered shock, affairs, shame, sin, rumour, anything at the edge of the unsayable. Let me carry this whole ancestral load like a pilgrim on an endless journey gathering firewood, milking goats, picking berries and planting seeds until the end of time. I am the seeker of your redemption, preserver of stories, telling your tales to the future. I am not yet old, but fellow, forever curious, often puzzled and sometimes thoughtless.

We don't remember most of our own lives yet my body remembers your trauma. I'm stuck in the wrong neural neighbourhood.

That tendency to marry too soon for the wrong reasons and to be honest, I almost did the same. That urge to leave home as soon as we could, whether running from or running to, the problem is always in the act of running.

Survival Strategies

for Mum

The door to the wardrobe hangs open. She can see as she walks into the bedroom that the thing is empty. Strange, the dresses keep disappearing, not returning after washday. There's a note on the bed from her mother addressed to the deli owner, saying she hasn't any coupons left, begs *could we please have meat, sugar, anything?* She pictures the woman, big palm opening, chest heaving. At the Archbishop's house they both kneel, kiss his ring. He speaks to them then, says he has need of someone to come in, cook meals for the hungry. Poor turn up to his door while her mother is in the kitchen cooking casseroles all day then takes the tram home at night. Dresses find their way back from the wash. The blue gingham is a size larger, someone else's name inside the collar.

The Fear of Hands

for Ellen Martin (Bebb)

They wander in to the old Cremorne smelling of fingers & palms. You can't see their faces beneath the rim of fedora & cloche. A poster on the wall swears there are no rats, no fleas, upon the tan bark stage set between awnings beaded with rain. Here in the open air the people spill mouthfuls of themselves while each hand is stung by the other's skin. It's where stars will throw down their light from the darkening sky and perish by morning only to revive night after night, like you. The floor- boards on which you walk, waiting for the music to begin, waiting for Stiffy, & Mo. He wears a boater, holds on tight to his boot, you singing his lyric, *black & blue, red hot & blue*. But tell me more of this night, of the backroom where you slip dance pumps over white silk tights, of that short satin dress, & mostly the hat of feathers – it wants to be flown like this. Say what's on your mind as each of you lifts a knee, perfect pattern of right angles, say why you are the only woman not smiling. A theatre full of hands & not one of them touches you.

Peace is a Room for One

Outwith the crow and cow, ranunculus
and everlastings, the outhouse is

grey and aging, a woman gathering
her long orange skirt into two

ruffled blooms, her face upturned
to the light in the crack of the door

inside this dim box of a place, bright
white cottontails brushing over

her thighs, as she folds translucent
tissue paper rosettes, scattering them

on the crazy bluestone floor. Her gut
contracts at the grind of loose stones

turning over in the laneway. She stills
her breath listening to the boys

rustling, pushing open the rear hatch
the night cart used. They slide in

a white gerbera on a long hairy stalk,
its puff adder stealth, its cryptic art

of being scentless, its many tongues
find her skin bare. Her screams billow

into the unsprung face of the ghost-
ing daisy, into its wide dark eye.

Minnie's affair with Squizzie Taylor

for Ivy Monica Minnie Bebb

Minnie was handy with her chip shop in King's Cross. The storeroom out back was full of his arms. As far as anyone knew, she peeled potatoes, cut them into rough batons, whisked up a batter, bathed fish in it. Her wide-mouthed grin chatted to the customers while she fried everything in lard. On open palms she handed over their orders news-papered in a tight swaddle, each bundle the shape of a newborn. Gangs roamed outside in the street but never opened her door. Not her door – too much confidence in her smile, too much gangster on her arm after closing. When she spoke, all the little daughters hung on her words. She was in my ear the night you & I sat facing each other for the first time at the Witch's Cauldron, us in the shadows of black hats.

Only a Teaspoon

i.m. Henry C L Bebb

Like me, she was never a practical kind of woman. She was all music halls and opera, playing violin in the bathtub or the rain. And love. One morning, as her man leant against the wooden railing of the old Queenslander, he took a breath then lost it again almost right away. All night long he'd been leaking sleep. Now he couldn't stop slipping in it. She was beside him, cupping an elbow in one hand, a teaspoon in the other. The first dose soaked into his brown tie. He still had plenty from his barrister days in London but some ties he'd never cared for. They were a rhyme for goodbyes. She had to leave her baby's cries for Brisbane's flies. He swatted them. At the roadside he walked and weaved, not looking back until he fell on a mat of rotting Jacaranda blossom. The gentle musk of purple panic[1] was all around. However brandy on a crumpled sack suit slurring in the gutter was the first thing the young sergeant noticed. By the third stroke it was eleven am at the station, and too late. If only policemen were detectives, or physicians.

1 Refers to the Jacaranda tree or 'exam tree'. In Brisbane, purple panic is a botanical symbol of the start of university exam time and student stress.

Cataracts & Dogberries

for Lena Munday Marlow Anderson

i

Thanks for the grapefruit. She's tapping to find the weak spot. My gift of books may as well be a sack of old newspapers. We play I spy with my little eye. She keeps saying *eye stye.* I mistake cloudiness for mirrored light, while she narrates a cryptic crossword from memory. You read her clue then read her again backwards, looking for the subsidiary. Go back to the beginning. When I say I could exchange the romance for mystery she inclines her head, asks *why, have you not noticed the waterfall?*

ii

I lay bare a hand-me-down mannerism—her closed-lip smile, an almost imperceptible shying turn. It scribes against our nihility. But there are other things. Some allude to a reckoned weariness—hands cupping cheekbones, the fall of the voice in pitch. At the foot of the bed a chart reads 'nil by mouth' & 'not for resuscitation'. With her kidneys shutting down, there'll come a flooding of the body, a thirst for air, an erratic heart. At the sound of my sigh she sits up, mimics my Duchenne smile.

iii

She hands me a hundred-dollar bill, explains how this is part of her last will & testicle. I let that slide to ask about the home of her childhood. *Oh it was a lovely hysterical house, you know, one of those with a spinal staircase.* I imagine polished whalebone with its vertical articulations between handrail & cantilevered steps. My right thumb and forefinger trace over the knuckles on my left hand. She carries on talking of how the house was haunted. *Quite a friendly spirit, you know, but we called the priest anyway, had it circumcised with incest.* My mouth opens & all her poltergeists swoop in. On my way out, I pass by the waiting room. Two small blonde girls are watching television.

another red-letter day empties its head

overlapping images • slightly missed focus • she is skin on darkroom skin • I bury her again under my finger • the pressing re-opens her front door • a back door opposite swings to the yard • *watch them chooks they swoop* • squeak of wire gate • my fist in her hand • one egg in the nesting box • two mouths burst open • *my name isn't lindy lou!* • voice like my sister's • cracks in the stone walls • all her tendrils & cape weed loose on the inside • red flowering gum leaves dropping • her birdbath is full of lips • hint of ginger from the students' studio window • sticks & bowls clinking • three shy faces grinning • nodding & sipping four o'clocks in the ripe sun • pink tea horizon • we are bougainvillea • wind blows us open • scattering over grass • small, pale, inconspicuous • wrapped in bright clothing • double exposure • her smile is a bow untied • cheek in one eye

Patterns, Inconsistencies and Microaggressions

Eight of us are seated at a long table by the window
our reflection superimposed onto a view of the river
so that we could be said to be in two places at once
despite the background noise and heat from the kitchen
anchoring us to the room, as if that were the collapsing
point, the necessary interaction with the real world.

Father is in a wheelchair, says he wants to be placed
at the end so he can get out quickly if he has a need
and I think it sounds like something I should consider,
especially today. I've had a difficult time trying
to get everyone to come together at the same place
at the same time. But our mirror images on the glass

show how we are still not quite all in real agreement.
My sister has her head turned away slightly. Her voice
is a study of politeness while her mirror-self moves
its eyes upward in an arcing motion from one side
to the other on the surface opposite, as if by some trick
of the light it has succumbed to Caputo's *strange face*

illusion – an error, my face-specific interpretation
system gone wrong. My blood pressure having risen
momentarily, falls again at the sight of our lunch
arriving. There's something endearing, equilateral,
about the *Coquilles Saint-Jacques* on their fan-shaped
shell which offers a brief moment of rightness.

Even its name printed on the menu is a darling. Mainly
I love how all of its looping consonants look like fish.
It's the same font used for the poem titles in Fish Work.
And isn't she also a darling for writing in it – I love
your work? My other sister drops her fork. My brother
notices something most fascinating under a fingernail.

Strange-Face-in-the-Mirror Illusion
Giovanni B Caputo, 2010. Perception 39:7, pp. 1007–1008

Possession & a Niggling Apostrophe

The midwinter sky had a puppeteer for a moon
when the little daughter was clamouring air
from her lungs, although the spider didn't fall

as so keenly anticipated, already tomorrow saw
her obsessively picking at split ends & she did
not like to be left alone on that front verandah

for the taking & did not want to be given away
as a trinket to the man with his bag of black
cats—how she clung onto you while you laughed,

she was inseparable. To keep yourself apart
from your family, you shifted into a tiny house
its dust settled in the breaches of your keratin,

the little bits of hair everywhere & your mind
became secretive about the places you kept
your handbag, how to put together a phrase,

about your growing inclination toward sleep
& even in the end she tried to hold onto you,
skin white on white like the lilies on the table

dropping petals, soft things not meant to last
long, & it was that finger-biting first child
who couldn't stop caressing the newly fallen

flower, who would accident across thoughts
that should never have been written down,
who held a photo of you bearing fairy wings

& the cheek-biting, the plucking of eyelashes
began again, & always a niggling apostrophe.
She'd once tried to tell you she was a keeper

of rituals & there have been so many times
she went to speak of this, the checking, the hair-
pulling, the compulsion to read & count letters

in threes. But you were never going to live, no
matter how perfect, how many repeats of three
she/cou/ldf/ind/iny/our/neu/rol/ogi/st's/rep/ort

Meanwhile, genes are deciding if they want to be read

Inside the pantry, there's a nail in the door where the calendar is missing. It finished in February, the month we received her diagnosis. I've nowhere to stick the reminders to check her personal alarm. There are too many appointments to scribble on a calendar anyway. Her daily ritual is kept in a ring binder, his in another beside the large plastic box filled with medications. I can't hear his reasoning for taking the wrong day's pills. Because the table is full we sit outside on stained seats, crowded by white-hooded peace lilies leaning in, holding up their little microphones. She's bending forward as if tying shoelaces, eyes closed, & I ask if she'd like to go lie down. She's says no, because I'm still there, sits up to reread the same newspaper she's been reading for days. I google *temozolomide* & find it causes mispairing of tumour DNA, reading it triggers futile cycles of excision & reinsertion of bases until it breaks, the cell cycle arrests, killing itself. Mum, I say, but my speech is patchy. It comes out sounding like um, like the sound you make before you speak. She was there with me prior to speaking, there before I learned to speak, there long before my lungs functioned in air. Her name is the sound of morning meditation. Sometimes when no-one's paying attention she's the spirit who wanders off to bask in the sun while my father climbs out of his wheelchair onto a park bench in a half-standing salute, trying to locate her. We're always failing to be in two places at once. I want to exist in duplicate, be more than I am, be my own child, the one I never had, a child who accepts a situation simply for what it is. My wants are too many & I'm sweating fish out here, tiny fish like commas in the silence while I think of something meaningful to say – a silence defined by the loudness of a plane, a small dog across the street wanting to be let in. Mum, I say, *anything interesting in the news? Not really, she says, nothing much new. It's like I've read it all before.*

Tea Minus Three Months

We keep missing each other in the house, as if our existences are separated by a severed particle of light. The collapsing point appears on the sofa where she opens her fist & liberates a hummingbird moth raining scales from its wings. *You know she used to wear all my clothes & I'd get so angry*, she says of her sister. For a third time I ask how she'd like to mark her birthday. She pulls a face. *I haven't given it much thought*, like it isn't going to be her last. Stormcloud on the back of her hand, she gathers both teacups & walks outside. It's so hot I can't see for heat waves. While her face yields nothing, her hand offers up another moth, its soft caterpillar body wailing like a kettle. I think of the woman, houseful of cold tea, leaving cup after cup on every surface &, unable to locate any of them, spends all day returning to make more. Outside, the tea is lost for colour. I find her overwatering the hanging pots of bee balm & many clear-winged moths scatter. As we hug, she hinges unusually close, our sheer blouses unfurling in the easterly wind.

Texting while Running Late for Day Procedures

Lullaby becomes *kill any*. I tell you Thursday cuts like a pillow leaves impressions on your face when you walk into it waxen skinned, & its satin edges angle through the hours tossing yellow mirrors into the afternoon. It takes me on impromptu elevations & descents, lateral extensions & velocities of hospital corridors where the only thing going on time is the sun, on a run between buildings, past coffee shops shrill with metal & steam, into the foyer random as a roundabout in a French village, into the white tent for its last-minute plastic stick up your nose. Everywhere there are sapphire-blue trousers & tunics, wheels, sticks & shoes, wheels, sticks & shoes. We wait wordlessly with mask, phone, sweat & surrender. She is still as an old clock, expressionless but for the slight movement of a hand on her face as if thinking to say something. Lift doors open in the distance & over there is a tiny blue fellow perched on the knuckle of her little finger for a second before flitting away. I'm trying to absorb everything as the day rushes by in & out of perspective. On pressing 'send' on a text, it occurs to me that I have her fingers. Two of them anyway, my forefinger & little finger, whereas all the others seem to resemble mostly my father's. *I think I've gone & left the vaccination certificate at home*, she says, underneath a sign labelled *Admissions*.

All the Gentle Planes are Grounded

'I know that from here you cannot escape by plane—you have to be able to fly on your own', Vasyl Holoborodko

She knew each plane in the sky, the time it flew over the house, where it was headed. Her life became focused on destination. Too late now to hold a serious conversation about how she might like her last days to pan out. She doesn't see the hurry, *the doctor says I have only three years*, like she will have to stop dancing due to weak knees. I can't tell if she's avoiding or not comprehending the reality of these final few weeks. It changes everything, and nothing. I get her to chat about her most memorable holidays instead. *Coming in to land at Hong Kong, passing a high-rise window, we watched a man inside ironing a shirt in his underwear.* There'll be no black box recording after she's gone. I want to extract her every remaining thought, try to think of it like wandering a maze of roads on a quest in some virtual reality, trying yet another lock with my sack-full of keys.

A round, bright light hovered ahead of the wing outside my window on a night flight, the odd angles, that way it sped off then returned. When I showed the flight attendant, she flung down the shutter, eyes wide as daisies. 'Keep that closed!' She stares blankly for the longest time before speaking. *I think I'm done with flying now.*

On the evening news, we watch Russian aircraft bombing Ukraine villages which cuts to rain bombing of Queensland which cuts to bird weather—an increase in the amount of meat in the air around city airports since lockdown & the rising risk of bird strikes. *If you become the light outside my cabin window, I say, or a plane-seeking bird, watch out for engines, won't you?* The only planes flying over my house now are Hawk Fighters from the local military air base—I think how only the wrong people are travelling.

Homecoming

'Once upon a morning I woke up being a bomb and flew headlong home' – Lesyk
Panasiuk

I wake again, eyes like pilot lights. My mother is still asleep in
the next room, but I'm not in the same house where I lived as a
child, & this does not feel like home. The bed does not feel like
my bed. When I roll over, my hips find hollows left by cycles of
children, & the only thing that sleeps is my arm. I'm here because
of the bomb wedged in her cerebral cortex. It's just light & I can
hear sustained whimpering.

She's curled on the carpet, wedged
between bed, table & wardrobe. I have never tried to lift an adult
off the floor before, the full weight of her carried on my thighs
& calves, my labouring breath. A tiny assassin sits on my palm –
round, white, waiting. Picture it navigating its way inside vessels,
the stealth of it crossing over the blood-brain barrier, lining up
its target, the rupture. Part of me breaks off, guttering & spent.
She sleeps away the chemical morning.

In the kitchen I am
burning myself on micro-waved oatmeal & banana. Exactly why
I am coating my tongue with sugar & pressing it to the roof of my
mouth, I can't recall. I'm hopping through walls, tunnelling-time
barely discernible. In one room she's small & I'm checking for
bruises hiding in her hair. In another, it's me who is small, ripping
the head off a plastic doll named Grindl, home going off inside
my hippocampus.

In the course of her erasure, a single joyous wish

Every time he speaks she dies a new death, not the staggering theatrical kind, but staggering nonetheless—a theft of all of her yesterdays, one unseemly denial at a time. Owing to Covid restrictions, only two people at any visit are permitted to enter the neurosurgeon's office but they manage an exception for us. Clutching a walking frame, my father shuffles in, following behind my mother and me. Her head scans are waiting for us, displayed on the computer screen. The workings of her mind have never been so intimately shared, the light spaces, the dark, the knot nesting in her frontal lobes like she simply worried it into being. The results and prognosis are clear. It's February, she won't see past May. We're asked if we have any questions. I look at her still beside me but there's no reaction. I'm anxious she hasn't understood. My hand opens but the first words spoken belong to my father. *So, what's going to happen to me?* To which the surgeon answers *you should be in a nursing home, sir.*

The next few weeks occupy a displaced time. I overhear him on the phone one afternoon, telling a friend about how *she died two hours ago,* while she's sitting up in bed, me spooning tomato soup from a cup. It takes me a few seconds to decipher the words. *What did you just say?* I honestly think I must have misheard. *Mum died two hours ago,* he says, as if repeating news from the television. *No, she didn't!* I yell it, unable to edit the outrage from my voice. He covers the phone with a hand. *Oh, she will soon though.*

As it happens the 'friend' is an enemy of mine—a drunk, aging, overweight ex-cop of the corrupt kind—and I can feel a vein popping. I recall wishing him to fall down the stairs outside his own pub, and he did. So there is that.

May 8th, Mother's Day, and she's in the bedroom as our family sits in the kitchen discussing funeral arrangements. Nice. Today will be all kinds of wrong. I ask to change the subject, suggest we all gather around her in the bedroom and talk because hearing is the last sense to go. Nobody moves.

My father isn't saying much, his teacup is empty. I wonder if the conversation has become too real for him, wonder what he's thinking about, wonder what he needs. So I ask if he knows how he feels about the idea of life after Mum goes. He raises his eyebrows, turns his palms upwards. *I suppose I'll have to find a new hobby.*

Every atom that was you

Yes, work now at pinning matter to spirit;
Do it even if you think it's just a quibble with the wind
—Medrie Purdham

I wanted a physicist to deliver the eulogy
            to say *no*
                        your energy has not left us, no
nor was it ever invoked, *de novo*
            at the precipice of birth
it was gathered, shaped into a constellation,
how, in its own way, it will go on
being transformed   a small part into light
            & then
right away there's something new assembling

            in this moment,

                        my concentration has waned
& it's in the following of the sun
                        through the window
I come to understand how you will continue
to throw yourself into me
surprised to find you already there

            in this streaming light, I can't tell
            if that's a helix of dust, a portal
            or a murmuration of small birds

            all of my whims

are yours   how you'd swim only before dawn –
that's when every still thing has its chance to move
for you   all that is ordinary becomes extraordinary.
This morning I thought I saw a cracked heart
emptying itself into a rock pool,
        three wan faces wailing at the sky.

Welcome swallows
          swoop insects above the lake mid-flight,
          swerving close enough to cause ripples,
how one object moves another without touching.

As the sun hangs her petticoats in lemon-
scented gums,
        sliding over their bare limbs
in the wind   that moves the leaves   that shift the light
in the mottled shapes dragon-dancing on the grass
I wait quietly for you to reveal yourself
      among a thousand butterflies, black

After the Funeral

I wheeled my father home to bed
to sleep off the whiskey
but he just stared open-mouthed
straight up at the ceiling
unable to describe to me
what he saw—
I don't know, I don't know…
so I sat in the house, waited hours
for my siblings to join us
as arranged,
how we would all be together
keeping him company
late into the cricketing night,
I don't know
but I kept texting, checking my phone
for answers, its bell
has a different sound now,
so I tied it to the cat
and left, and I will keep leaving
and no-one will ever be honest
with themselves.

Afterlife of a Housecoat

'for cornflowers to sing they must be fallen'
—Susan Fealy

Show it to me, your cotton summer
housecoat, white, blue cornflowers,

once hanging on the hook fixed
to the back of the painted bedroom

door, & which I've laid flat at the foot
of the old double bed, unbuttoned,

open at the front, sleeves spread out
ready to slip on. The night nurse,

she said it was too sad seeing it limp
where you'd left it, too sad for him

to be facing the unfilled smock
as he opens his eyes in the morning.

She was wearing this only yesterday,
she said, when she ordered me to go.

A strong lady your mother!
I could tell the gesture she used

was a direct copy of yours. Show it to
me, not her, your morning peignoir

& tell me how it's possible that you're
able to take this with you, this look,

this lasting self-image. Was the wrap
simply handy, or does it feel homely?

All these rooms we are folding into
boxes, everything you've touched

except for the housecoat I'm thinking
to air on the clothesline, in the sun,

a breeze to help you out of it &
into transitioning the three bardos[1]

& a rebirth. Today is only the half-
way point between the previous you

& what comes next, & you're still
quite yourself, leaning on a wall

as he sleeps away, then taking tea
on the patio, reading the newspaper

while you wait for him to join you,
one wet thumb held up to the wind.

What am I to do with the housecoat,
this singular supplement to your body,

this symbol of a life lived in the home?
Maybe I'll pass it to a sister or a cousin,

in the manner of Emily Dickinson's
white house dress, cotton with mother-

of-pearl buttons, that lived on in her
bedroom at the family homestead.

After the last lockdown, in your retreat
from the outside world, you, in your

terror that you also could tell no-one[2],
abandoned the habit of changing

into day dress, as the cold virus raged
across the land. When was it that

you wore the housecoat for the final time,
if ever there will be a final time?

I've half a mind to tear it into fourteen
pieces & fling them over fields,

its printed flowers, like little blue gods,
ever resurrecting amid the growing corn[3].

1 Bardo (Tibetan) is the transitional process in between lives
2 From Emily Dickinson's letters regarding her mental illness
3 Resurrection of Osiris, Egyptian God of the Afterlife

Improbable Acts of Proximity

i
To imagine the dead are running
short of space—I'll call it unlikely, so much of it
going spare, idle, we're most hectic at the edges.
I hollo long into the wintering acres, white
particles of grief touching a thing that hits another thing
hurtling towards an edge. You bring spectre only to strangers
because my longing is too great, my pull too strong.
At some point the moon will spiral in so near,
our ocean tides will tear it apart, & it will be sublime,
for a minute.

ii
When minutes go backwards, we will
return all this chaos to order, this drinking glass
will suck wine from our fishly mouths,
we'll throw soft ash into the flame, watch you emerge & all go
home. My message bank returns us to June,
there's a sound like the wind after you stop talking,
a beep. I keep on replaying your last call—its temporary
queering of time that will go on to shrink & stretch. Our cells
are just a clock on repeat, wound to fifty cycles or so.
Our baby teeth are full of historical hours.

iii

Toothpaste goes back into its tube & the man who broke
science can show time flowing in two directions,
& how people are so easily fooled. Take a drunken mind-
photographer & the way he projects his thoughts
onto Polaroid. Pictures in my mind remember the future.
In it, I'm in two states at once. It's chaotic there & you are
there, waving as if you know you're being watched.
Stare at a waterfall long enough, rocks begin moving upwards.
It rained on the night you rose in a panic & flew.

iv

My blousy mood is bicuspid, a rose crossing boundaries
with a peony. It's been an extraordinarily untidy time
with relationships, obligations & bouquets
& the vagaries of opiates meet my anxiety
about premature burials. A worried little bird
wagging a tail at the gate, curious to see who turns up. You,
forestalled on the other side of time,
finding a way to reconstitute. During the oratory,
white Madonna lily buds are giving birth
to tiny ballerinas, feet first.

v

Unfamiliar days are emerging & sky,
having removed its cast is paler underneath,
less muscular. We don't know yet what we're capable of,
other than translucence. These blurred hours
belong to the edge. Once again, my mind wakes to a fall,
it doesn't know which part is gone, like a missing arm
keeps reaching. I steep some extra-strength
tea, this is how we know each other best,
what we substitute for love you & other words
that don't sound right when held in the mouth.

vi

Our mouths are barely acquainted,
& elbows in a cramped room—a series of hip hellos.
The long eyes & their languishing ability to bend light—
it strikes at odd angles. Shapes often resemble faces,
I forget that I've seen inside you. In the womb
I first saw the colour red as a kind of nebula,
a star dying in its own web, & a thing so immense
out there, if I climbed out too soon, I'd collapse.
Faraway things, if suddenly fetched in too close,
I, like a broken bone that heals, would never be the same.

Portrait of Marie Theresa

for my mother

She was
fur *Elise* in a box
sugar flowers & tipsy fruit
jitterbug, jive & do si do
far-flung
& a scrap of
fight the father

Where fragile things meet ordinary air

It's me who's thrown. He holds up the image to the light box,
pointing out the lack of hands and feet, the amphibious stumps.

Pectoral limbs extended laterally, the ventro-dorsal position
gives an impression it came into the world ready to fly. *Foetus*

– born without a head. It was blue, he says, flashing the
radiograph. *It looks like a frog*, I wail, both hands hovering over

my mouth. Hanging out of the waste bin, a heat-proof, foil bag
from the rotisserie chicken he'd x-rayed out of boredom. Our

giggling is interrupted by a caterwaul coming from the street
below. Through the timber sash window I notice a span of roof-

tops. When I look a second time, beyond the point of focus,
I see a mother from years before, her stricken face hollering

at the bedroom door, an aunt calling over and over, unable to
reach the doctor. Outside, I'd been watching a father filleting

raw tadpoles on a rock, to place upon the tongues of us children
for the leap factor – an athlete's secret. He was busy plucking

four little gaping mouths from the goldfish pond in the moment
a breathless, blue baby wrapped warm in a blanket went quietly.

Something amiss in the carrying

'...*your body quiet having spilled its secret*
your palms flat on your belly holding holding...'
—Amit Maimudar

I'm not worried about crushing in crowded doorways
or being chased by dogs, since I am not a sheep, yet
bending here in this window-less room I am shedding.
The water in the ceramic bowl, full of movement
like fish – sudden mass of tattered red tailings spiral
a few moments before dispersing. *Panic.* I can't help
looking for signs of molar hair or early fingernails but
no, none.

Already the disassembly to single cells
begins. You're falling apart. Kandinsky's *capricious* forms
hold tight to their positions as if there'll be no letting
go. The slow leakage of salt across. Both of us
powerless at keeping the inside in and the outside out,
we go into osmotic shock. Vacuoles pump to ditch
water as it rushes in, overwhelmed by the flood,
spilling jelly and small skeletons or trees, their harvest
of oddly-shaped fruit.

Baby you're a phoront, carried
into groundwater, into the pores and crevices of rock,
soil, roots of the citrus tree beside the tank, into flesh
of the fat blood orange I will eat one wet morning
with breakfast, cross-legged in shorts on the sun-
venturing verandah, ripple of bright juice let loose in
the air, rolling over the curvature that is thigh.

Evacuation

On the night of unpeopling, scent of ash ruptures sleep. A siren
sends a colour wheel of greyscale, red, blue, on skin, on walls.
The room is loud with *leave now, leave now.* Outside the man with a
bullhorn is turning to smoke. I fill a bowl of water for the willie
wagtails. Our four-wheel drive is packed with dogs, five days of
underwear, a stack of poetry books. We breathe into our shirts,
head down to the lagoon where young men circle us on the silent
street, looking for opportunity. More displaced arrive. Families sit
in cars, watch the future unfold on iphones. All roads home are
blocked by police. On the round-about we keep going round. At
four am the early morning moon throws light on all that has gone,
leaves a side of itself on the hill.

Letting Go

We squat at the edge of the river, our fingertips poking out from sleeves of an oversized jumper – its belly-full of liquid amber leaves. Teenagers bounce each other off a seesaw, a car horn loose on the bridge, the rolled-up jean cuffs damp against my legs. Talk of the guy we tipped out of a canoe by accident. My dog swims out too far and returns with a green bouquet between her lips, a remnant of last summer's algal bloom. You climb a tree, release all of autumn upon me.

Our Closing Narrative

to Marc

It was the place of our slippage,
flower by the porch – the lavender, the love ender –
we made excuses for the withering
                moved it all out to the verge
on the day the old man next door left
sprawled on the floor of his kitchen
            the box of rolled oats, the broken bowl
how the timing made us pause. That evening

           I watched my hand passing
the ring back to you across the table
and you said *not now*, that way
you always did when you really meant *wait*
          while I take control
and I remembered it's what you said
when the ring was made and I was longing
to collect it from the jeweller

                 not now, not now, but already
the sky had grown over the places we stood
dead-heading roses, and where the tree dahlia shook
                with bees – their cantillation
less animal than words
the way they limped between us,
and when you said I *don't know what to say*
to an empty wine glass,
a crow answered

Menstrual health—no data, no cycles logged

It feels like hate.
The wind outside is groaning, lifting a little
the open window—as if
it wants to come in. I'm breathing the hurt air

like an argument with a sort-of friend
who doesn't care for me or my ear
for Indigenous *Voice*. My neck hurts.
There's always an injury on the left side.

Parasailer in a corner of pale grey sky,
above the pine tree, its branches
lined with hands cupped upwards, waiting
to catch him, or maybe it's just ordinary

exasperation. The dog is barking again
because it's now six am
and I am still in bed, in my head a polemic,
same old bone thrown into relief—

let's say we are invaded tomorrow
forced to speak a foreign language and we don't
even recognise the weird alphabet,
next your children disappear, your home,

then might you understand? Sort-of friend
does not unfold her arms, does not
look at me, does not even answer
and seems to hate me now, it feels like hate.

The floorboards where I walk are creaking
so much I'm wishing I had an eating disorder
but I'm just too damned hungry, and itchy.
My app tells me this could be normal.

I feel like I might be going to cry—
the dog, her dark eyes, the sofa streaked red,
cushions in pieces, the wall's flaking paint
and it feels like hate.

Everywhere I tread I'm stooping to wipe spots
of bright red blood off the shiny tiles,
(even fucking Facebook ads are mocking me)
but my cycle tracker knows this blood isn't mine.

And that bitching wind, troubled thing,
would have me swing from the high branches,
bones flipped to the outside of my body
my umbrella skin folded up inside.

Dysesthesia

Transforming the medical record into poetry

There was a burning of skin
in the *dermatome* under my left arm,
& I was changing
into a long white cotton gown
with ties in the back

& I am back, slipping
into my first laboratory coat
as a doctoral scholar in a new lab
—I'd been used to them buttoning up
at the front, & it felt momentous
somehow,
    as if anything could happen

The radiographer, there to capture
the *herniation, degeneration,* the *osseous lesions*
of my *cervical* bones,
to make drawings with the rays, the shining,
exposes my neck to the eye of the scanner
        & dashes out of the room

My *annulus,* my little ring,
like growth rings on a tree, on the scales
of a fish, a doughnut, a halo,
        (anyhow smaller than an *anus*)
calcifying, falsifying, overlying, mystifying,
      misidentifying
is hardening to stone

The table lines me up in the tunnel

& the x-ray tube inside the gantry
 buzzing, clicking, whirring
makes tomographs in thin slices as it draws

Hold your breath
 Breathe
 Hold your breath
 Breathe

By the way, my lung's apices,
much like small rods at the top of a flamen's cap—
 the priest's emblem of the shepherd—
apparently are as normal
 as air is black.
Sitting up to leave, my right hand extends
as if it expects to be kissed

'In the crotch of this fig tree, starving to death'

Title borrowed from *The Bell Jar*, Sylvia Plath

When you take to my hands, I ask how you see yourself held
—an insect, a ripe fruit, a dog's ear?
                                        You say,
some days I might be a tree that needs pruning, or a man-
dolin with an extra string—somehow capable of things
far beyond my ordinary potential.

        I sense something exotic about the supernumerary
string, as if the mere tenor of it might send one falling
into a death-like sleep.
                        I suffer soft auditory illusions
in the night, a vague ticking in the walls, a sound like stars
dropping out of the sky one by one to the earth—put simply
a lone gratuitous loose wire arcing wild with disconnect.

A sudden rattle of dry leaves, a thousand tongues clicking,
mocking all belief that we have crossed a mortal boundary.
Are we so perilously superhuman in this wind?

I look around at the tree for a casting of untimely figs,
you bring me back to the moment. Sliding onto the back
                        of my hand is your sun-ripened hand,
curved, consonant, a vein pulsing.
                                Say your palm is edible.
If it *were* a fig, I would know right away that you were
ready to consume—slightly soft with a strong sweet smell,
with only the smallest of bruises, a few brown spots, a light
wrinkling of skin. I could feel its willingness to break.

—I think how a wasp has to die inside a fig for it to mature,
the female enters an opening so tight it peels off her wings,
the flower liquefies her with ficin, feasts on her entrails—

You talk about a study on reading emotions from hands,
squeeze my fingers,
                    you're a baby bird, unfeathered, hungry—
I twitch and counter with nesting insect, suffocating.
This makes you release my hand,
                                        at first a blanched fist,
mottled pink and white, its subcutaneous wiring of small bones
and vessels. When it opens, you place in it a fig, inverted.
                    Here, can you eat this?
I tell you I can
                    see myself feeding in the flower of your eye.

from the Ruffled Edges of Carnations

Carthusian pinks, skeletons with lipstick kisses
              smudged, we were warm and flushed
      the day we became possessed by the light
scattering at sunset, the time we were taking the waters
        from a lake so near the sea, salt crystals appeared
        in the form of cubes,
the edges scratching away at our skin
us relishing the cracks and the crevices in the salt
derived from bodies
              of water that dried up centuries ago.

I would have painted my mouth for you,
          not like a model in some glossy magazine,
more like a tiny crimson dianthus in a meadow,
              loose, ethereal and pleasingly wild.

Our conversation is coloured rose with the rustling
of leaves, the lapping of waves
on the beach, of steady rain, the pink noise
        of heart valves opening and closing.

I deaden my own inner noise to listen for you,
I sing to you, I pace
         every day over salt-crusted ground with you,
talk over old memories with you
have everyone around us loll to the ground
         in mad-honeyed silence.

I'll perform a thousand dry-runs in my head
          until there are no more mistakes,
a shot of clove on my breath, tell you *yes*,
         tell you this as if you are really there.

Self Portrait as Sound

from 'Avalon', the legend, and song by Roxy Music

Close-mouthed, I still feel conspicuously loud. Soft hum surrounded by paisley etched on indigo so loose it occupies the volume of a seat, spills over beside a crumpled can of synthetic caffeine and sugar on the floor with two fraying oven mitts—a commuter's discarded grasp on home. A rogue cloud keeps pace with the train, and I'm full of found rhythm, a repeating song I keep inside.

Out of my head, I say, I do not want your isle of the dead or your perfect red apples on close-clipped grass.

A nurse calls to tell me that my father is shut down, not very responsive this morning, and I know that maybe he's just plain tired of moving his larynx, the illusory, yet real, sensation of shouting, of the sticky blue recessive colour that passes through generations, narrowing the lumen of throats and grows over the opening out of which would otherwise escape the shame of being audible. It's the way vocals take up so much more space than the body, the contents of a mind wandering inside the heads of others, old trespass, that old childhood crime of being heard unbidden.

I'm so tired now the train has stationed. The song lets go of my lungs, my rusted chatter, my blooded craw. As I open my mouth, apple blossoms shoot from sleeping wood.

Sketch Poem of Fireworks at Dawn[1]

So soon, having lost too much of herself,
Mother is folding her hands underneath
a noise in the night sky shedding white light—
      confetti on fire, a small peony
      inside a larger peony burning.
Afterwards it becomes nothing but smoke
and there is nothing left to hit the ground.
When the spark is gone, she shrinks, depleted
back into her arched body, letting go
of all that she has been holding onto.
How wretched, if at the quell of a star,
none of us was altered by its rattle.
Woman with white lashes, raking her hair,
singing to *life is not a waiting room*[2].

1 Song title by Senses Fail
2 Album title by Senses Fail

Synesthesia through Binoculars

(When I thought I saw the Green Comet
but it Was Only a Shooting Star)

We took off beach-side to escape the trees
the air warm and doughy, the foretelling
swelling in our lungs like leavening bread.
We were circling beneath the hunter
when I became distracted by your face—
how it held all the light of a street lamp
one second, shadowless, nothing to declare,
and a loose hound the next, the angled eye.
In the clearing we stood heads tilted back
gaping at the comet's gas trail sweeping
its cold-eyed arc across the sky. The ice
clatter of emerald against my teeth,
a trace of mint in that one fine moment
you opened and swallowed it, tail and all.

Sonnet for New Beginnings

Black night, made of faraway suns & cries,
folding white terns into the limestone dunes—
her tissues tucked into a nightshirt sleeve.
Everyone who knows her knows everything
in which she sleeps is white on white on white.
Watching her disappearing into light,
I'm suddenly unnaturally tall.
There are wrong-coloured apples in the bowl.
I'll have to count the coffee beans again,
& all the perfect round things must stay round.
The moon, ripe & light, rolls from the tree top,
& drags its long, soft tongue over the sea.
The persistence of old stars as lanterns,
as net of unimaginable days.

Watching the Lightning Strike

Come is the day light leaves a birdless place,
nuclei of heavy atoms blasted
into the cloud by an exploding star,
and let's say the light pulse could look outward
from the nucleus—it would see a field
of faster time, and you might see a freak
mirror of yourself. You can't look away.
Silent rays are sparking from sky to skin—
star-light synapses faster than a thought
shower down on the welkin of the earth,
pass right through us while our eyes are smitten,
and doesn't this change you, doesn't this change
the way you evolve, how it edits you,
the way you're read, one letter at a time.

Poetic Constellations

An Exploded-Sonnet Sequence[1]

Triolet

Have you ever wanted to skin
a star a thousand photons deep
to know the colour of its eye?
Have you ever wanted to skin
a cell just to watch the turning
wheel of the universe within?
Have you ever wanted to skin
a star a thousand photons deep?

******

i Olbers' Paradox

We are stars passing into light,
into light, into light. More stars
between us and between them, more.
We will never have enough time
to create enough stars to keep
us bathed in infinite starlight.
That younger universe we see—
it's watching the birth of the moon.

ii *The Night the Moon Transits Leo*

The dark sky opens its windows,
slowly winding its stony clocks.
Tonight, I harvest my pumpkin
in the waning old of the moon.
A spider hanging in the air,
a waxen moth trapped in orbit,
it glimmers like a longing eye
against the wild nocturnal sky.

iii *The Universe Repeats Itself*

The galaxy sways on its tree,
with a hum from one still struggling,
a sound like the low frequency cry
of a captive star succumbing
to a black hole's own wailing song—
a longing from the potter's field—
this star could be a wingless moth
pulled lax to a ravenous mouth

iv Our Lady of the Falling Star

On the brink of unwanted love
became a bird and threw herself
into the freezing sea below,
halo of stars around her head,
a trail of seaweed behind her.
The fig leaf tail of a runaway
left to twitch and wag, arc and fall.
It will wink out if you chase it.

v Supernova

The night is barren, the storm is
still faraway and the air is
light on my skin. It's a great night
for the splitting of nuclei,
for cosmic rays to shower
into lightning, the exploding
star's reminder that the breaking
can seem gorgeous from a distance.

vi *Our Galaxy Tastes Vaguely of Raspberries and Rum*

The rare spice of a shooting star
leaves a sense in your mouth of toast
and a light herbal bitterness—
the taste gives a high note to beer.
Water returns to its lowest point.
Look up at the backwards question—
this out of season meteor
comes like a lonely drop of rain.

vii *No Red Dwarf Has Ever Died*

Out of the peel of blackened sky
I'll make you a box of darkness
with a screaming star in its heart[2],
a young star prone to temper flares—
it will burn for a trillion years.
Think of me as you watch it rage,
consider why it's beautiful.
I don't know what else to give you.

Sestet (for the Splitting of Nuclei)

This out of season meteor
with a screaming star in its heart,
and a hum from one still struggling
left to twitch and wag, arc and fall,
it glimmers like a longing eye
passing into light, into light.

1 Sonnet consisting of an octave (triolet)
and sestet split apart, the sestet reseeding
a series of seven new octaves
2 External seeding from Mary Oliver
and a Terrance Hayes sonnet

87

The Hum Hearers

for John (Paddy) and Jessie Green

I touched the glass. The thunder told me to. It opened my ribs
and touched me back. I want to say *vibration*. Sending memos

to my past self, feet up against the window, I let the rain drive
its bass notes into my chest—like that ceaseless hum of Earth,

or the sound of an old queen with her cluster of bees looking for
a new home, a forefather and his harmonies dead for more

than a hundred years—his *dear boyz, dear boyzz*. I want to say
synchronicity. Dear me, remember the day our ancestral mother

returned with lit cigarettes, two long-stemmed glasses pressed to
her unbuttoned blouse and we careened, arm-in-arm, wine-

breathed into the city? We were going to lose ourselves there
outside a Celtic music club, to long-ago lungs of the Highland

pipes—it was enough to listen, a few east wind nettles catching
on us. I want to say *embodiment*. We were each of us without

tether, timing continuous, that trance note beneath the notes, the
drone that is never silent. We danced spring-beat-beat,

wheeling around, stopping the moment the piper took a break
and just like that it was over. She shot a cone of crimson light

out of her eye and disappeared. It was like looking into the sun.
I want to say *fluctuation*. The way we travel in and out of time

via sound. I begin to hear the noise of this world again, water,
one note at a time in the gutter, the moon ticking in a tree.

Acknowledgements

'The Hum Hearers' (unpublished manuscript): Dorothy Hewett Award 2023 (Shortlist)

A selection of these poems: Unberthed; Untimely Fruit; Let me run a salt bath for her, burn some sage, chant; Taking photos of strangers after breakfast in the crypt; Liaison at Evans Music Hall; Sunset Salad; Bathing in vinegar & leftover wine; If a Flower Could Be Called a Waif; Out of Failing Bodies, appears in: The Blue Nib Chapbook 6, 2020, Chaffinch Press, Dublin; Winner of the Blue Nib Chapbook Competition 2020

Instinction: Meanjin Quarterly, vol 78.4, Dec 2019

Lost Wax: Westerly 64.1, July 2019

Only a Teaspoon: Poetry d'Amour Anthology 2019

Letting Go: 1st Place, Creative Connections Poetry Prize 2019

Inhabiting the Tesseract; Repurposing a Bleed, and Kandinskyesque appear in: Science Write Now 2020, 2021

Evacuation; Any Skin but Our Own; Old Man Who Spits Pearls; appear in Of Moon and Sea, 2020.

Another red-letter day empties its head: Stilts Journal 8, 2020

Our Closing Narrative: Meanjin Quarterly 80.1, Autumn 2021

A Sum of Spectacles: Westerly 66.1, June 2021

Cataracts and Dogberries: 2nd Prize. Fish Flash Fiction Competition & Anthology 2021; and YouTube https://www.youtube.com/watch?v=vAaVRHompAw

Sequelae to misplaced elbows & other violations: Shortlisted, MPU International Poetry Competition 2020; Longlisted, Fish Poetry Prize 2022

Where fragile things meet ordinary air: Westerly 66.2, November 2021; Shortlisted, Australian Catholic University Poetry Prize 2021

Shooting Cloud at a Sky: Shortlisted, Silver Tree Poetry Competition 2022

Patterns, Inconsistencies & Microaggressions: Westerly 67.1, 2022

Possession & a Niggling Apostrophe: Australian Poetry Journal 12.1, 2022

Afterlife of a Housecoat: Highly Commended, Ros Spencer Poetry Prize 2022

Tea Minus Three Months: Shortlisted, Bridport Flash Fiction Prize 2022;
appears in the Grieve Anthology 2022

Texting while running late for day procedures: Shortlisted, Bridport Flash
Fiction Prize 2022

Every Atom that Was You: Poetry d'Amour Anthology 2022

Homecoming: Grieve Anthology 2022

All the gentle planes are grounded: 'Poetry of Encounter', Liquid Amber Prize
Anthology 2022

Improbable Acts of Proximity: Runner-up, Gwen Harwood Poetry Prize 2023;
first published in Island 167, 2023

Triptych with Oranges: Cordite Poetry Review: No theme 12, 2023

From the Ruffled Edges of Carnations: 1st Prize, Poetry d'Amour Poetry
Competition 2023; Poetry d'Amour Anthology 2023

Poetic Constellations; Watching the Lightning Strike; Synesthesia with
Binoculars; Sketch Poem of Fireworks at Dawn, were commissioned by
Perth Writers Festival and Westerly, and first published in Westerly Online:
djinda, November 2023

Self-Portrait as Sound: Westerly 68.2, November 2023

Menstrual Health – no data, no cycles logged: 3rd, Tom Collins Poetry Prize
2024

Dysesthesia: Island Online, 2024

The Hum Hearers: Finalist, Joanne Burns Microlit Award 2024; in Remnant,
Spineless Wonders, April 2024

Exploded Sonnet Sequence: Best Australian Science Writing 2024

Sonnet for New Beginnings, Quadrant, 2024

BIBLIOGRAPHY

C. Backster & S. G. White. 'Biocommunications Capability: Human Donors and In Vitro Leukocytes', *The International Journal of Biosocial Research* 7.2 (1985): 132–146.

Dias, Brian & Ressler, Kerry. 'Parental olfactory experience influences behavior and neural structure in subsequent generations', *Nature Neuroscience* 17 (2014): 89–96.

Perroud, Nader, Eugene Rutembeza, Ariane Paoloni-Giacobino, Jean Mutabaruka, Leon Mutesa, Ludwig Stenz, Alain Malafosse and Felicien Karege. 'The Tutsi genocide and transgenerational transmission of maternal stress: Epigenetics and biology of the HPA axis', *World Journal of Biological Psychiatry* 15 (2014): 334–345.

Phelps, Elizabeth & Hofmann, Stefan. 'Memory editing from science fiction to clinical practice', *Nature* 572 (2019): 43–50.

Rich, Judith. 'Healing the Wounds of Your Ancestors', *Huff Post* (2011). Sourced at: https://www.huffpost.com/entry/healing-the-wounds-of-you_b_853632

www.ingramcontent.com/pod-product-compliance
Ingram Content Group UK Ltd.
Pitfield, Milton Keynes, MK11 3LW, UK
UKHW040732200225
455358UK00001B/23